better together*

*This book is best read together,
grownup and kid.

 akidsco.com

a
kids
book
about

a kids book about WAR

by Sarah Jones

a
kids
book
about

A Kids Book About books are available online: *akidsco.com*

To share your stories, ask questions, or inquire about bulk
purchases (schools, libraries, and nonprofits), please use
the following email address: *hello@akidsco.com*

ISBN: 978-1-953955-65-4

Designed by Duke Stebbins
Edited by Emma Wolf

To all those who entrusted me with
their stories and allowed me to bear
witness to their truth.

Intro

No matter how old you are now, there have been wars happening around the world during your entire life. And as prevalent as they have been throughout history, the concept of war hasn't gotten any simpler or easier to talk about, especially with kids.

The reality of war is that it's ugly and it's complex. As grownups, we can often try to protect our kids from the world's harsh realities because it's more comfortable to pretend no harm can ever come to them. But kids are more resilient than we realize. They're curious and ready to talk about big things, even if they're scary. And wars will continue to be a part of their lives, so the more they can learn and have space to ask their questions, the more empowered they will be now and in the future.

The goal of this book is to aid in making the conversation about war more approachable. This book also creates space to think critically about what starts wars and why they keep happening, and what we can learn from our past to create a better future.

Hi. My name is Sarah and this is a book about war.

You might be thinking...

*War is such a big topic—how can you write a book on it? Especially one for **kids?!***

Well, you're right...

There's no way I can share *everything* there is to know about war in this book.

But what I can do is help you understand a few key things:

what wars are,
why wars start,
how wars work,
and **whom** wars affect.

But first, let me share a
little bit about myself...

I'm a journalist, which means I share
news about things happening around
the world to keep people informed.

Sometimes, that means traveling
to other countries, telling stories about
what has happened or is happening there.

Like covering a
presidential election.

Or covering the spread of
the COVID-19 pandemic.

But sometimes it means going
to places where war is happening,

reporting on what's developing,

sharing stories about the people it's affecting,

and helping the world understand ***why*** it's happening in the first place.

There have been **MANY** wars throughout history.

So war means a lot of things
to a lot of people.

And it can also cause
a lot of *big* feelings.

HOP

Like...

ANXIETY, ANGER, SADNESS, and even ELESSNESS.

What do you feel when you think about war?

It's totally normal if you feel scared and confused, because war is violent and it's complicated.

My hope is this book helps you understand
a bit more about war and why it happens.

Because when we understand
something better, it helps us
manage our feelings about it.

So the first big question to ask is...

what exactly is war?

As simply as I can put it, wars are
fights between groups of people,
usually about who gets...

POWER.

Wars are usually fought between 2 or more different countries.

But sometimes they can be fought within just one country (that's called a *civil war*).

When countries fight using words,

it's called **DIPLOMACY.**

But when those fights use weapons instead,

it's called a **WAR.**

Beyond the definition though,

WAR IS
BRUTAL
UNFAI

UGLY, AND

Wars cause destruction and pain.

And no matter how a war is fought, people almost always die.

You might be asking then,

why do wars happen?

The main reason wars happen is **power**.

You may hear that wars start because of **religion, ideology,* resources, strategy,** or maybe **territory** or **land**.

But at the end of the day, it all comes down to power.

*Ideology means a set of beliefs.

Power isn't always bad!

Sometimes people use their power
for good to help others.

Other times people freely give it away so others can have more freedom.

But power can be bad when the people in charge make harmful decisions.

Decisions like who gets to be

HAPPY,
SAFE,
or
FREE...

and who doesn't.

War might seem like a big idea
that's really hard to understand.

But something I want you to know is that war always involves...

PEO

PLE.

Real people,
with real lives,
and real names.

During war, people fight
each other with weapons.

The people doing the fighting are
usually soldiers, but not always.

Not every soldier fights with weapons.

Some do things like cook or
come up with strategic plans.

Wars also affect people who aren't soldiers—even kids.

And I think you should know
that people die in wars.

No matter how they're involved
and even if they don't want to be
involved at all.

Houses get destroyed.

Hospitals can be bombed.

Kids aren't able to go to school.

Sometimes people don't have access to things like running water, food, or a safe home.

Sometimes people live as refugees in camps for years, and they can be separated from their families.

Sometimes the only way people can be safe is to move to a different country where they don't know anyone and don't speak the language.

As a journalist, I've talked to so many people who've experienced this side of war.

They usually love and miss what their country was like before war happened.

They'd go home in a heartbeat if it was safe to do so.

But many times, that isn't an option.

Wars can last for days or weeks.

More often, they last for months or years.

But wars don't last forever...

so how do they end?

Wars can end with a compromise, or a peace treaty, where all sides agree to give and take.

Wars can end with the formation of a new country (like the United States).

Wars can end with a change in leadership.

But even after a war ends, the effects don't just go away.

WARS CAN LEAVE COUNTRIES IN DISAR

They can leave people scattered
all over the world.

They can leave people feeling
angry and bitter.

And people who feel angry or bitter about
wars might start new wars years later.

Did you know that right now,
somewhere in the world,
there are wars happening?
It's true!

Usually when a war starts, a lot of people around the world talk about it and care a lot about what happens.

But after a while, some people just get used to it and stop thinking about it as much.

That doesn't mean what's happening is any less dangerous or bad.

It just means that other countries don't think it affects them, or journalists from around the world aren't all being sent there to report on it anymore.

I don't think this is right, but it does happen.

This is some heavy stuff, right?!

It's not easy or fun to talk about.

But it's so important for you to know.

Why?

Because there *will* be more wars.

And those wars will continue to hurt countries, grownups, and kids.

In all likelihood, people will continue to fight over power.

And there will always be people who do good things *and* bad things on every side.

I've met with people who have lost everything because of war.

And even in their pain, when they have close to nothing left, they have always welcomed me with whatever they could.

The thing that keeps me going is remembering these people.

The ones who selflessly do good for others even in the most difficult situations.

THEY
ME

GIVE

HOPE.

So let's not forget about the people who war affects.

They have names.

They have families and friends.

They have dreams.

And they're just like you.

Outro

Starting the conversation is often the hardest part, so thank you for taking the first step. This book isn't meant to tie up all the big questions nicely with a bow, because frankly, none of us have all the answers. A lot of complicated feelings and further thoughts may remain. And that's OK. And if they don't, that's OK too. All feelings are valid.

If the kid in your life wants to dive deeper into the topic of war following this book, here are some questions you can think about together:

1. What are you feeling right now?

2. Is there anything that still confuses you that you want to learn more about?

3. Is there anything that worries you?

4. How can we help those impacted by war?

When a war breaks out, news coverage can be non-stop, and the violence and destruction can feel overwhelming. Encourage your kid to talk about how they feel, write it down, or draw it out. And remind them they are safe and loved and there is always reason to have hope.

find more kids books about

imagination, anxiety, racism, money, body image, failure, gratitude, life online, optimism, empathy, and emotions.

a akidsco.com

share your read*

*Tell somebody, post a photo, or give this book away to share what you care about.

a @akidsco